Living Life
After the Fires of
My Sorrows

REBA HARRIS
With Seant'a Conyers

Publishing Services By: Pen Legacy, LLC (www.penlegacy.com)

Library of Congress Cataloging – in- Publication Data has been applied for.

ISBN: 979-8-9860732-2-4

PRINTED IN THE UNITED STATES OF AMERICA.

Dedications

I want to thank God for allowing me to become an author at the age of 81. I also want to thank my late husband, Oscar Harris, for his support in this endeavor, though he was unable to see the finished product. My aim in writing this book is to encourage others who may feel they have nothing important to say. Their story may be just what another soul needs to continue in this thing called life.

I would like to thank John and Patty O'Donnell for their financial support at the beginning of this vision. When so many people did not believe what God had asked me to do, they believed in me, and for this, I am truly grateful. The Gilead House would not be the place of change if they had not come alongside me and invested in God's vision for His daughters. Thank you both from the bottom of my heart for your faith in me and what I am called to do.

When others suggested to me on numerous occasions that I should write a book about my life, I wondered who would want to hear from someone whose life was as unimportant as mine. But after being reminded of how many miracles God has performed in my life, I decided I wanted others to know how God uses ordinary people to do extraordinary things! I owe it to tell the world that even though He may be calling them to pull away from the crowd and step into their calling, He knows what He's doing…even when we don't. Trust God, anyway!

Thanks to my first writing coach, Benita Tyler, who started on this journey with me, and Seant'a Conyers, who came along and helped me see this journey through until the end.

To my readers, as you navigate through life, I hope you find this book useful, and I pray no matter what, you won't give up until you reach where God has called you to be—in His Kingdom.

Table of Contents

I want you to believe you can rise above your past. Listen to more of what is inside of you, instead of what people say about you. God said, "You will hear the voices of culture, but learn to obey the voice of God."

Living Life
After the **Fires** of
My Sorrows

Introduction

My name is Reba Lynn Johnson-Harris, born 1940 in a barn my parents converted into a house to live in with my brothers and me. My mother was Luetta White, a bi-racial woman; my father was Leonard Johnson, a Black man.

My mother was born when the law still supported segregation. Growing up without being accepted by neither Blacks nor Whites made life painful for her. Even in today's society, bi-racial people say they don't fit in, just like my mother. See, Caucasians dislike bi-racial people because of their darker skin, and Blacks don't accept them because they're too light. This same issue affects a lot of Blacks in our own homes. There are brothers, sisters, and other family members who dislike the "light-skinned" ones in the family, typically because they're a darker shade themselves.

I grew up under the *Jim Crow* laws, which enforced racial segregation in parts of the United States, including public facilities such as schools, transportation, restrooms, and restaurants, even trickling down to drinking fountains. (The laws were invoked in the states of the former Confederate States of America and some others beginning in the 1870s and were enforced until 1965). Because of Jim Crow, Black children had to attend their own schools. I remember my Black classmates calling me "yellow" because I was so light. Some children even said they disliked me because my skin was lighter than theirs.

Living Life After the Fires of My Sorrows

Unfortunately, today's society still determines a person's character by the color of their skin.

The Beginning of My Sorrows

W hen I was born, my father was so excited that I was a girl! My mother, on the other hand, was not so happy. She always stated that if she ever had any children, she did not want to have any daughters. Well, there I was.

I never knew my mother's reasoning for not wanting a daughter until during an eight-year journey to heal from the childhood trauma I suffered. I discovered she had been molested numerous times while living in foster care and believed I would be subjected to the same fate. Her fears kept her from loving me. My mother failed to realize that her rejection and verbal and physical abuse caused just as much pain in my life as she had experienced in hers. After marrying my father, my mother hoped for a better life. All she wanted was someone to love her, but life failed her again.

I was the third oldest of six children—four boys and two girls. Three years after I was born, my mother gave birth to my brother, Fred. Three years after he was born, my sister, Karen Kay Johnson, came along, looking far more White than she did Black. Like my mother's side of the family, Karen was pale with a head of sandy brown hair. Unfortunately, Karen and Fred became terribly ill with whooping cough; my sister did not survive. She was only two years old when she died.

I remember the night Karen died vividly. Earlier that day, my mother had taken her and Fred to the doctor. By sunset, my mother experienced trouble with her bowels and spent most of the night running back and forth to the restroom, so my father took Karen to the hospital. After a few hours passed, he returned home, crying hysterically. Through his tears, he finally told us Karen had died. Her body was brought back to our house, where she laid in a casket in our living room for three days. Every night, I got up and went to pat her stomach, the same as I did while she was alive, to help her fall asleep.

After the loss of Karen, my mother told my father, "I need another baby to help me heal." I could tell Karen's death devastated her and how much she truly loved her. Honestly, I believe my mother loved my sister more than me because she resembled her side of the family, and I didn't. In the midst of her grief, my mother eventually got her wish. I learned my mother was pregnant, and that is why Dad married her.

Dennis was my mother's favorite out of all her children. He looked just like Karen, with pale skin and sandy brown hair like my mother. She loved him because he also looked more White than Black. In fact, out of her six children, my mother only liked three of her children: my brother Leonard (the oldest), Karen, and Dennis, who became Karen's replacement.

Similar to me, my brother, William Larkin (the second to the oldest boy), also had a painful experience growing up with my mother. William and I were her least favorites. My mother didn't like brown-skinned men, which is why I'm not sure why she married our father. William was our father's shade, which caused my mother not to like him…just like me.

My brother Fred was different from the rest of us. He shared something in common with my mother: They both had a difficult time learning. Since my mother had difficulty learning herself, one would think she would have been more understanding of Fred's disabilities. However, she was more worried about him being made fun of at school like she had been while growing up.

One night, my mother whipped Fred because he couldn't spell a word as she told him to. As cruel as it may sound (and you're probably thinking maybe he could've spelled it right so she would have stopped whipping him), my mother's motive behind the spanking was to keep the kids at school from teasing him.

Through all of this, my saving grace was my father! After Karen's death, I was the only girl in the family. My brothers used to say I was my father's favorite because he wouldn't let them hit me. Now I realize it was because he knew my mother treated me differently than the boys, although she never mistreated me when he was around. The only problem with that was my father wasn't home much.

My father was a womanizer. He had women in and out of our hometown of Marion, Indiana. The way he mistreated my mother made her miserable and unloving. I had to understand that she was never loved correctly by her husband, had been abandoned by her father, and lost her mother at nine years old. None of this is an excuse for treating me the way she did, but I see why. But back to my father.

My father was a happy-go-lucky man, well-liked with loads of friends. By contrast, my mother had very few people she liked enough to consider friends, except for Marge, her best friend, who was like an aunt to me. Since my mother was not very loving, not even towards my father, he sought companionship and love outside of our home. My mother knew he was involved with other women, but with no job and five children, there wasn't much she could do about it.

Despite us being extremely poor, my father was a great provider for our family. There were gifts for Christmas and baskets for Easter, and we were well clothed and fed. Our clothes came from rummage sales; I went to school dressed like my brothers in blue jeans, red sole shoes, and a plain shirt, all of which came from rich people.

Because my father consistently worked two jobs, we always had a place to call home. He worked at a hotel, had a cleaning job at the bus station and a bank, and also worked at a factory pouring hot iron. Later, he retired from RCA (Radio Corporation of America), the place that made televisions.

I remember the one time when my father took my brothers and me to his cleaning job at the bank. I don't know how or why I ended up with the key to the bank, but on the walk home, the key fell out of my hand while I was swinging my arms, and I lost it.

When I made it home and told my mother what happened, she said, "Your father is going to beat your ass!"

Have I mentioned that my mother was a cussing woman? She cussed us children out every day.

By the time my father made it home from work

that night, I was in bed. He came and woke me up.

"What happened? How did you lose that key?" he asked.

I was so terrified all I could do was cry. I cried so hard that he had a hard time understanding what I was trying to tell him.

Once I finally recounted how the key came up missing, he just looked at me and said, "I'll tell the bank, and they will have to change the locks."

I was in shock. He didn't whoop me! But he went on to explain that he would probably lose his job. I found out later my father wasn't mad at me for losing the bank key; he blamed himself.

"I had no business making my children be responsible for that key," he said.

Our father didn't spank us often. He was always more concerned about us fighting and hitting each other. He didn't like it. Whenever he caught us arguing, he would say, "If anyone's going to be doing the hitting around here, it'll be me!" He was adamant about not spanking us and fussed when our mother put her hands on us. So, she waited until he wasn't home to slap me around, then dared me to tell him.

I never told my father about my mother hitting me or about the time she made me sit at the kitchen table until it was time for me to go to bed because I refused to eat my food. Why didn't I confess that she was abusing me? Because if I did, he wouldn't be home to protect me from her.

School Years of My Sorrows

Growing up, I attended D.A. Payne, an all-Black school, for seven years. We had one teacher, Miss Nevada Pate. The restrooms were outside, and since Miss Pate was assigned to teach eight different grade levels (which was virtually impossible), class was seldom held.

"If I can teach them to read and do math, I think they can make it in this world," Miss Pate used to say.

When I made it to fourth grade, Miss Pate

allowed me to help her by teaching the first, second, and third-grade students everything I had already learned. In the meantime, my father helped me with my own studies, namely math and spelling. He even helped me practice my spelling words on Thursday evenings to prepare for Friday's test.

Every year, Miss Pate treated the eighth-graders graduating from D.A. Payne into high school to a trip to Chicago for the weekend. Back then, Blacks were allowed to stay at hotels in Chicago, but not in Marion, Indiana. Since my last year at the school was seventh grade, Miss Pate took me along with the eighth-graders on the trip. Knowing my situation at home, she also helped me out by letting me stay with her sometimes on the weekends.

There was a nice school down the street from where we lived, but my siblings and I weren't allowed to attend because it was all-White. Once, my father set up a meeting with the school administrators, trying to convince them to accept the kids from D.A. Payne. Of course, they denied his request. Although he had a desire for his children to do better than him and my mother, most of the opportunities we sought were blocked due to the color of our skin. We were denied countless conveniences others had.

For example, Blacks weren't allowed to attend Matter City Park, where the public pool was, so we went swimming in the river until my friend, Cletus Cobb, drowned trying to swim across it. We couldn't go skating at Idle Skating Rink, either. As Blacks, the only place we were allowed to have fun was Webster Park, where we went to play, make potholes, and lances that went around the neck.

Eventually, D.A. Payne was shut down, and its students were transferred to Central, an all-White school where I completed eighth grade.

My eighth-grade year at Central was bittersweet. Mr. Detro, my teacher, was a nice man

29

and an excellent teacher who taught me well. I was the only Black student in my class; however, the White girls liked me and asked me to be a cheerleader. And even though I can't carry a tune, I was invited to sing *Ave Maria* during our graduation ceremony. The audience endured my joyful noise the best they could. Between Mr. Detro helping me learn as much as possible and the friends I made, eighth grade at Central turned out to be a wonderful year. But as much as I enjoyed school, things at home took a bad turn.

That same year, my parents constantly argued. I remember one time my mother called the police on my father because he had taken all the locks off the house windows. She eventually projected her fear onto me, saying things like, "Your father is going to kill us!" I was confused because my father always treated his children better than he did his wife.

Once he had enough, he moved out of our house.

Living Life After the Fires of My Sorrows

When I visited my father at his place, he cried and begged me to ask my mother if he could move back home. My mother refused. They divorced, sold the land and the house, and divided the money between them so my mother could pay cash for the longed-for house she had been wanting for many years. By the time the divorce was final, my two oldest brothers, Leonard and William, had joined the military, leaving Fred, Dennis, and me alone with my mother. Though my father wanted me to live with him, I couldn't because I was responsible for watching my two youngest brothers and keeping the house clean while my mother worked.

Teenage Years of My Sorrows

Following my parents' divorce, my mother relocated us to the upper side of Marion, Indiana, where I enrolled in McCullough High School in 1957. The following year, I transferred to Marion High School. During this time, my mother worked at Marion General Hospital in the kitchen, and my father had a brand-new home built down the alley from where we lived. My two brothers and I commuted between our parents' homes, easing the tension for all of us. Every day, my mother came home from work, fixed supper, then sat on the couch nursing a cigarette in one hand and a cup of coffee in the other while I kept the house clean and babysat my brothers.

We were seldom allowed to leave the house, and when we were allowed, my mother instructed us to stay in the yard. There was a time a tornado tore through our neighborhood, destroying Martin Boots Middle School, where my brothers attended. The misplaced junior high students transferred to the high school I attended, cutting our classes to half a school day, four hours for each grade.

One day after completing my morning classes (my brothers attended in the afternoon), I decided to play kickball in my neighbor's yard. Time got away from me, and before I realized it, my mother had gotten off work. I got in trouble for not doing my chores, and she made me deep clean the entire house by myself. That night, I wasn't allowed to go to bed until I had taken all the dishes out of the cabinet and washed them. Once I was done with that, I had to clean the windows and whatever else my mother thought of for me to do while she sat on the couch smoking.

As I completed my chores, I thought back to the day in divorce court when the judge asked me who I wanted to live with. I clearly said, "My father," but the judge told me, "No!" My mother cussed me out the whole way home, then got on the phone and called all her friends, telling them what I had done and calling me all sorts of inappropriate names a mother should never call her daughter. She wasn't mad I hadn't done what I was supposed to do; she was angry that I chose my father.

In high school, I had a small group of friends. One friend came from a very affluent Black family who lived in a nice home. She was very light-skinned, and a lot of the black girls did not like her. But my friend accepted me.

When I turned sixteen, I desperately wanted to

go with my brother to a place called The Center, but my mother always said no. Around this time, her best friend, Marge, was a saving grace for me, just like my father. Aunt Marge knew how my mother was mistreating me. "Why are you so mean to her?" Aunt Marge would ask her. After a while, she convinced my mother to let me go to the youth center with my brother.

One night at The Center, I was hanging with my brother when I ran into my friend, Janice, who married Frances Jefferies at eighteen. Janice told me that she and Frances were having problems in their marriage, and she had decided to file for divorce. As closing time approached, Janice and I stood outside discussing what she was going through. While we were speaking, I noticed Frances stalking from behind the building. With me standing right next to her, Frances walked up to Janice and began shooting! He shot her six times, then ran off!

I froze in place, screaming. Some of my male

friends heard the commotion and ran over to see what was happening. They picked Janice up and rushed her to Marion General Hospital; she died before they made it there. Frances ended up serving prison time for her murder.

I met Oscar Harris at The Center. He was nineteen and from Kokomo. Oscar was cute, and every girl at The Center liked him, but he approached me to go and hang with him at a different spot than everyone else was going to. I ignored him and went straight home.

The next day at school, my friends informed me that Oscar was talking to them about me and sent his number for me to call him.

"I'm not calling him. He has too many girls liking him," I huffed.

Three years later, I met Oscar again. I was nineteen, and he was twenty-one. We began dating and later married. Oscar and I were married sixty-one years.

I had some good friends in high school. There

was Carol Jones, whom we called Tootie. Then there was Birdie and Tyrone, who married young, started a family, and are still married today. And I can't forget Sally, one of the smartest girls I knew.

After Sally, Judy, and I graduated high school, we all took the nursing entrance exam. I was the only one who failed. Judy and Sally both passed, went to college, and became nurses. I was so proud of them! I also had many male friends who looked out for me and made sure I wasn't mistreated. Aunt Marge's son, Donald Stewart, was like a big brother to me. Then there was Tyrone, Corky, and a few other male friends who took care of me, too.

After we married, Oscar and I moved to Kokomo, around the corner from Earl Davis, a male friend who I grew up with. Earl moved to Kokomo around the same time as me and opened a barbershop. Other classmates like Johnny and Larry Bowles and the Perkins girls lived down the street from us. The Perkins girls were so beautiful!

They were very light-skinned and put together and came to school dressed in fine clothes. What I wore to church on Sunday was their everyday wear.

I always thought women like the Perkins wouldn't accept me as their friend because I was out of their league; however, they did. We were so different from each other. I was poor and did not dress as nice as them. In fact, I dressed like a boy, the same way I dress until this day.

I enjoyed school, but growing up poor made me feel like I wasn't smart enough. I felt like an outsider around my friends whose lives were better than mine because they had mothers who cared for them.

Reasons for My Sorrows

As I grew into adulthood, I started grieving over my parents' painful 25-year marriage. The healing process took me eight years, but it helped me learn a lot about my parents. I thought the world of my father, Leonard, but he wasn't who I thought he was. He had done horrible things to my mother that I knew nothing about. And my mother had been molested so many times that she hated men.

My father was never given the opportunity to meet his biological father. His mother married

Ervin Johnson, who raised him, and I grew up thinking Ervin was my biological grandfather. He was good to us grandchildren, but my father wasn't very nice to him. I never understood why my father didn't like the man who raised, provided for, and accepted him and his children as his own.

When Grandpa Ervin died, my father did not attend his funeral. No one even told me that he died until two weeks later. I was devastated! Grandpa Ervin was good to my brothers and me and deserved to be shown respect and love. Once I found out he had died, I immediately apologized to his wife and three daughters for not attending the funeral and expressed my condolences.

My other grandfather, Peeler Ealer White, was my mother's father. A violent alcoholic, he never had anything to do with my mother and her sisters. He got married at a young age and had several children. He made and sold moonshine for a living and spent weekends beating his wife in drunken rages.

Grandpa Peeler had one son who fought him off his mother when he beat her; my mother and her sisters ran away until the fighting stopped. My mother's mom died when she was nine years old, so I never got to meet her. My mother's brother chose to pass for white, leaving home after my grandmother died. My mother and her sisters never saw their brother again.

After my grandmother passed, Grandpa Peeler's two oldest daughters, Agnes and Lavone, reported him for selling moonshine to the police. He was arrested and sentenced to nine months in prison. While he was in prison, Agnes and Lavone took care of my mother and their youngest sister, Dorothy. Knowing he would come looking for them when he was released, Agnes and Lavone took my mother and Dorothy to stay with their White neighbor and left town. Those neighbors kept the girls for a while before contacting CPS (Child Protection Service) to report they were there.

After CPS took them, my mother and Dorothy were placed in a home with Mother Julies, a Black woman who ran a boarding house. I am unsure if Mother Julies knew what my mom had suffered at the hands of men because my mom was an extremely withdrawn, quiet child. At the time, Dorothy was a cute three-year-old, too young to remember the violence in their home. She was Mother Julies' favorite.

While writing these words, I realize how much I've missed not having a mother who cared for me, like my friends. I have no memories of her taking me shopping like a mother and daughter would do. My father took me shopping before I learned how to shop for myself. As I grew up, shopping became an addiction for me. Even after moving to Kokomo and starting my own life with Oscar, I still felt like an outsider who didn't fit in.

Oscar had a lot of friends, both male and female. Most of them accepted me as soon as we met. However, I still felt insecure when I compared myself to these beautiful women who wore makeup and always had their hair done. They were more sophisticated than me and were afforded luxuries I didn't have as a child, such as roller-skating, swimming, or normal things kids do. While they were out having fun, I was stuck at home taking care of my little brothers. The only memories I had to share weren't anything I was proud of.

Before moving to Kokomo, Pearl Bassett, a hairdresser in Marion, taught me how to be a lady and helped boost my self-esteem. On the outside, I may have looked like a lady, but I felt like less of a woman on the inside.

I thought marrying Oscar would give me the social life I dreamed of, especially since I hung out with him and his friends often while we were dating. However, once we said "*I do,*" things changed drastically. Our wedding was on June 27th, and by the 4th of July, nothing was the same.

"I'm married now," Oscar told me. "I don't like to be around people, and now that I have a wife, I don't have to go out to meet girls."

I had no clue how much that statement would affect my sixty-one years of marriage.

One thing that drew me to Oscar was the way he treated my family and how nice he was when we were dating. In my mind, I set out to be a perfect wife, balancing motherhood and housekeeping with a healthy social life. However, reality turned out to be the complete opposite. Working hard to please my husband and be a good mother sent me spiraling into an addiction to prescription drugs that spanned twenty-three years. As I dealt with my addiction, I treated Oscar like a king, thinking he would reward me by sometimes taking the children and me out if I did. I was wrong.

My plan to be a perfect wife and mother failed miserably. Instead of things getting better, Oscar isolated himself. Now I did have the social life I desired, just not with my husband. Oscar never stopped me from going places, so I took the kids to carnivals, swimming, and the skating rink...without him. When I asked Oscar why he didn't want to go out with us, his curt response was, "I have work to do around the house!"

Despite staying home most of the time, Oscar did attend the kids' school functions. Of course, he wasn't happy about going, though. Oscar even sat in the truck during our son's little league baseball games. There I was, sitting in the bleachers yelling and cheering the kids on during the games by myself, even though he was right there. This was just one of the many sacrifices I made, and I was growing tired.

Oscar's past relationships with other women sparked jealousy, lack of trust and control, and seriously began affecting my marriage. I was drained; I dealt with my misery by taking prescription pills for extra energy. It wasn't long before I became dependent on them. My addiction became so bad that I was being "treated" by four different doctors in four different cities to get my pills. I wasn't sure who or where to turn to for the help I needed to be set free. At nineteen, I gave my life to Christ, yet I still could not seem to kick those pills. I was ashamed of being an addict and prayed every day for God to help me…then went right back to my pills.

In 1983, God delivered me from prescription pills. But soon after I quit using, I fell into depression. I ended up trading the pills for food, an addiction I still struggle with today. I gained over one hundred pounds and turned into a lonely, married woman.

Oscar was a nice, hardworking man. When he and I married, we had three rules: no cursing at each other, no hitting, and no affairs. Both of us honored those commitments until the day Oscar died. Oscar was saved and knew who God was, but he hadn't healed emotionally from his rough childhood. And although we both stuck to our marriage rules, we still had other problems.

My marriage had a lot of suppression due to Oscar's lack of feeling loved as a child and insecurity as a husband. His way of "dealing" with his issues was isolating himself, which made him constantly suspicious. Once that happened, he became controlling, and all trust was lost between us. Fear ruled Oscar's life; he didn't know how to deal with it. Nothing I did was enough to please him, and absolutely nothing brought him joy or happiness!

In the early stages of our marriage, we struggled badly financially, so Aunt Marge offered for us to stay with her family. Oscar defiantly refused, declaring there was no way we would ever live with anyone else. Honestly, I was happy Oscar turned Aunt Marge down. I didn't want to move in with another family; I always wanted my own home. So, we stayed where we were, managing to scrape by. Oscar had bills he had let go unpaid for over three years, forcing me to take a job at Howard Community Hospital to help pay off his past debts.

Oscar was working at Chrysler when I met him, which reduced some of our financial burdens. At the same time, he also helped his family out. He had a hard time refusing anyone who asked for handouts to a fault. His generosity was stressful because those same people he helped weren't there for him when he needed it. None of Oscar's family even came to our wedding. We invited all of them, but none came. Oscar was hurt; I was furious!

On the day of our wedding, Oscar's car broke down, and none of his family went to pick him up. Coincidentally, his friends Earnie and Janet Beard were on their way to the wedding and happened to see Oscar standing on the side of the highway. They picked him up and brought him to me. Oscar arrived thirty minutes late to our wedding. Not only because the car broke down, but because he was nervous about marrying me. That day, I learned that being late was Oscar's way of avoiding stress. His family didn't support him the way he supported them. They would spend all of their money partying and traveling, then turn to us for help when experiencing a financial crisis. Oscar couldn't count on them to do the same.

A few weeks following our wedding, we drove to Missouri to Oscar's grandparents' house. When we arrived, we walked into the house, and I greeted everyone with a hearty hello! Oscar's grandmother greeted me, but Grandpa Butler glared at me without speaking.

Once he realized who I was, he exclaimed, "I thought you was some old white woman!"

Oscar's grandmother never said much to anyone; she simply walked around mumbling to herself. Probably because there were rumors throughout the family that Grandpa Butler was courting a lady friend who lived down the street from their house.

Asking Oscar to treat us to a weekend vacation

was frustrating. "We can't afford it," he would argue. We didn't have the money when it came to that, but Oscar didn't mind traveling to Michigan to visit his father and stepmother or going to Missouri to see his mother. When we did travel, Oscar wouldn't take us to the zoo or any other family outings. We stayed in and occasionally went grocery shopping, unless his father took us sightseeing.

During one particular visit to Michigan, Oscar's father took us to see the new house he was building for his third wife...who was White. Seeing that house made my husband furious; his father never had a home built for him and his mother, Josephine. He mentioned there was one house he and his mother lived in for a little while but said his grandmother, Susie, constantly reminded him that her house was not his house. Oscar's dad built it, but it was not for Oscar Jr. and his mother. It was for his grandmother, Susie, who was Freddie's mother. I always enjoyed our trips to Missouri to visit Oscar's mother, especially hanging out with Uncle Perk, his wife Ruth, and cousin Geraldine. Oscar loved his uncle like a father.

Uncle Perk didn't live far from Oscar's grandparents in a two-bedroom government housing complex set up on cement blocks. Perk didn't have much money but had work done on the home, including building a small room onto the kitchen. He drove tractors and picked cotton for a living. Since he didn't start school right away, Oscar's mother took him to the cotton fields with her to help them work.

"That boy needs to be in school," Uncle Perk told her.

When Oscar finally started school, he was behind the other kids his age. He may have been late getting started, but Oscar loved school because, as he put it, "Going there kept me out of the hot cotton fields." He never cared much for spending time outdoors in the blazing sun. Even up until the day he died, he didn't like being outside.

One year, I had an above-ground swimming pool installed in our backyard. All the years that we had the pool and as many times as our children and grandchildren played in it, Oscar only used it once. It seems like many people grow up with the mindset that vacationing or relaxing makes you lazy. Oscar felt this way, and it caused problems in our marriage.

As the years went on, I was hired by General Motors. After starting work, my desire to go on vacations grew stronger. I listened intently as my co-workers discussed their adventurous weekends and holiday vacations with their families. Excited, I went home and told Oscar about the vacations, but he refused to go with me. I was always teased that my Caucasian side was provoking me to want to participate in dangerous activities, take wild vacations, attend a play in Chicago, go on a cruise, or go skiing with some of my co-workers from

General Motors.

"Please, Oscar, go with me!" I pleaded, wanting him to accompany me on a ski trip.

"It doesn't make sense to slide down a mountain on two pieces of wood," he grumbled in response.

So, when our children were old enough, they went with me.

I fondly remember taking a seven-day skiing trip with General Motors to Switzerland. Skiing, white-river rafting, and horseback riding were just a few of the fun activities we did. As usual, Oscar stayed home, saying he had work to do around the house. While I was away, I called home to check on him, but he would be upset with me. See, he never wanted to go, but Oscar didn't appreciate me going away without him. That's when I realized the only way I was going to please my husband was if I centered my life on him and our children.

Christmas is supposed to be a joyous time for

families. Growing up, I may not have had a loving mother, but Christmas time was fun at our house. We received lots of gifts, ate good food, danced to music, and my mother and father's friends would come over to visit. It was the only time we came together as one big happy family.

I desperately desired to have that same holiday cheer with my own family once I married, so I went out of my way to make it happen. I decorated the tree, cooked a grand meal, and decorated the house. But, Christmas made Oscar extremely depressed. He was so distraught that he pushed his gifts aside without opening them on Christmas Day. Each year, the closer it got to Christmas, the more depressed Oscar became.

"We didn't get much of anything for Christmas when I was a kid," he confided in me one day. "If we were lucky, we got fruit stuffed in a sock."

Oscar grew up living with his grandmother and his father, Freddie Harris, since he didn't want to move to Chicago with his mother,

Josephine. Oscar often asked if I thought Josephine believed he didn't love her since he chose to live with Freddie. I tried explaining she understood why he left to go live with his father, but no matter how many times I told him, he cried and fell deeper into depression.

Oscar used alcohol to cope with his pain and feel accepted. I understood how different his childhood pain was from mine. My mother may not have loved me, but at least I had my father and siblings who cared, whereas Oscar was an only child who always felt alone.

As time went on, Oscar's suppression grew worse. I needed to find something to help me cope with his depression and overcome my own issues at the same time. Thank God, I joined a women's group and started taking classes on healing my damaged emotions to find my joy again! The other women in the group took me under their wings and picked up where my mother dropped me off. Octavia Davenport, Edith Johnson, and

Sister Louise Bradley. All three of these women told me how they wished I was their daughter and treated me like I was. They taught me how to be a lady, care for myself, carry myself with respect, and find my voice.

As a young mother, I needed breaks from daily chores, taking care of the children, and tending to my husband and our home every day. I hired a babysitter just to get out of the house for a few hours. I ended up going to spend time with Octavia Davenport in the office where she worked for Dr. Richard Bowling. She had me help her out in the office, but she was such a great help to me, especially in helping me overcome rejection from others.

I cherished my time at Dr. Bowling's office. Octavia was a fantastic dresser and showed me how to be feminine. Dr. Bowling taught me to help others and not worry about what they thought of me. Being around the two of them was what I needed to overcome rejection.

I was a Wayman Church member for fifteen years before joining Mt. Pisgah Missionary Baptist Church. At Mt. Pisgah, I met Dennis Johnson and his wife, Edith. The Johnsons had two sons and a daughter who had passed away. They took to me like I was one of their own. Since Oscar knew the Johnsons, he approved of me spending time with Mother Johnson.

During one of our conversations one day, Mother Johnson said, "If I had another daughter, I would want her to be just like you." I had never felt more accepted and loved.

I needed Mother Johnson's comfort when my son was stillborn at seven months because Oscar isolated himself and wasn't there for me. He refused to view our baby boy Anthony's body after his death and later regretted it.

Edith introduced me to her good friend from Ohio, Louise Bradley—a wonderful chef and decorator. We became close friends fast. As she grew older, I drove Louise to Ohio to visit her family, and in turn, she pushed me to be successful and helped me accomplish many of my goals. The love I received from Louise was both a gift and a curse.

When my children graduated high school, Louise dropped by my house and cooked a five-course buffet to help us celebrate. The more she loved on me, the more people disliked me. She was not a well-liked woman herself because she looked White, but she was a good friend and role model to me.

One evening as we drove back to Kokomo from Ohio, it started getting dark, and I wasn't sure which highway to take. *What do I do, Lord?* I prayed. No sooner had I finished praying, I heard horns blowing around us, and I looked up to see two of Mt. Pisgah's vans! God answered me. One of the vans pulled in front of me, and the other behind. By the grace of God, I followed them on into Kokomo, and I couldn't stop smiling.

Driving Edith and Louise around are some of

my favorite memories. I felt appreciated by the two women I considered mothers and wanted to return the favor.

The Emotional
Healing of My Sorrows

Emotional healing is the ability to acknowledge events and circumstances in our lives that may hinder us from moving forward. After fifteen long years of marriage, things started to change for me. I was miserable, and my emotions were out of control. I needed healing! One thing I found is that along the path to healing, we experience five stages. First, we deny there's a problem. Next, we become angry. Then we bargain with ourselves, depression takes over, and finally, we avoid acceptance.

Emotional healing is a process that allows us to take control of our thoughts, feelings, and emotions. I realized I had nothing exciting in my life to look forward to except shopping, working every day, and taking care of my home, children, and husband. Around this time, my daughter entered the Miss Teen talent show in Gary, Indiana. My cousin Sara Lewis's daughter entered, as well. So, we all drove to Gary together. Everything that week was going wonderfully until Friday night before Saturday's finals when some of the Gary girls stole my niece Annette's outfits at dress rehearsal.

Not only were Annette's things stolen, but none of the contestants from out of town was allowed to practice with the pageant musicians. Only the girls who lived in Gary practiced their routines at the venue. My daughter was devastated that she didn't get a chance to practice her solo. My heart ached for her.

That Friday, the girls arrived back at the hotel from rehearsal at 10:00 p.m. I had already gotten ready for bed and was dressed in a nightgown, housecoat, slippers, and a head full of rollers, but when our girls let us know they had not had a chance to practice and that the director was waiting in the lobby, I charged downstairs and got right in the director's face. I yelled so loud that I drew the attention of everyone down there, and I didn't care.

Going straight up to the musician, I screamed, "If you screw up tomorrow when Shari's singing, I've already told her to stop!" Then I turned to Shari and said, "You put that microphone to your mouth and tell the audience how you and your cousin have been treated as loud as you can. You hear me?"

After my threats, my daughter was miraculously given the opportunity to practice before the show. The musician played beautifully for her solo, and she came in third place.

A few weeks after the talent show, Shari received a phone call advising her that she'd been moved up to second place because the girl who won first place dropped out after discovering she was pregnant...by the talent show director's son. Needless to say, after that confrontation in Gary, I found the strength in my voice deep down inside me. And when Oscar and our son came to support Shari in the show, they met a brand-new wife and mother.

While at the talent show, I came across a magazine article offering a deal on a four-day, all-inclusive trip to New York (except meals) for two hundred dollars. After all the drama that had gone down in Gary, I needed to get away! My brother agreed to watch the kids so Oscar and I could go to New York, just the two of us. However, soon as I told Oscar how much the trip cost, he denied me as usual. Of course, his reason was that we couldn't afford it.

Remember, Gary, Indiana, changed me into a

different woman. The new Reba Harris had a voice and planned on using it!

When my husband said no, I looked him straight in his eyes and said, "You may not be able to afford to pay for it, Oscar, but I can! And I'm going to New York, even if I have to go without you."

My friend Jean said if I went on that trip by myself, I might come home to all my belongings packed up and left on the front porch of my house.

"If that happens," I told her, "I'll take my things and get my own home to live in."

Needless to say, I went to New York by myself. Oscar drove me to the bus station in Indianapolis, where I joined ninety-eight other Black passengers.

In the midst of all those strangers, the lady I sat next to asked me, "Are you traveling alone?"

"I am," I answered.

"Are you running away from home?" she wanted to know.

I thought for a moment before replying, "I need

a change—to do something different with my life because what I've been doing for the past fifteen years is causing me to die on the inside."

I was so relieved when the woman looked at me and smiled. It felt good to get my feelings out.

I won't lie; the bus driver was attractive. He flirted with me the entire New York trip, but I did not go out with him or anyone else while in the city—only the other women I came with. When I got back, Oscar was still fuming over me leaving in the first place.

Always honest with Oscar, I confessed everything that had gone on with the bus driver, including his offer to take me sightseeing around New York. I even told him how the gentleman asked why my husband wasn't with me. That's when Oscar confided he felt our marriage had problems and that some days, he didn't know if he wanted to stay in it. I listened quietly—the new woman I was not really caring if he stayed or left.

Going to New York alone only strengthened

me to use my voice more. While I was there, I saw the *Jackson 5* play. I was so inspired that I told Oscar when the tour stopped in Chicago, I'd be going there to see it with the children and stay overnight. As I typically did, I extended an invitation for him to join us as a family. And for the first time, to my shocked ears…Oscar said YES! His agreeing to go on that trip opened up new opportunities for us to see other plays as a family, mostly in the Indianapolis area.

On one occasion, I asked Oscar for two weeks straight to take me to Bloomington to see Dionne Warwick in concert. And for two weeks straight, he said no. I was distraught, but suddenly out of nowhere, he agreed to go.

"I really enjoyed myself! I'm glad we came," he had the nerve to say when it was over.

Now he may have had a good time, but I was livid. I wanted to punch him and knock him over the second-floor balcony for making me beg him to go in the first place. Working that hard to get him to spend time with me was exhausting.

Thank God for me being obedient and listening to God's voice telling me not to attack Oscar; our situation seemed to improve! Before I knew it, we were attending plays with friends and dropped in on a few parties at the Carver Community Center. He even started playing basketball with the guys.

As things at home got better, General Motors offered me an EAP (Employee Assistance Program) position designed to help GM employees handle their personal and family problems. Based on my good friend Chuck McCoskey's referral, I secured an interview and accepted the position.

Listening to the employees pour out their hearts was rewarding because I love helping people find community resources to improve their lives, which in turn allowed me to discover there was more I could do to improve my own.

During my last ten years of employment as an EAP rep at GM, I served the people the best I could while I began preparing for retirement. It was time to go back to college and obtain a degree so I could work at Saint Joseph Hospital's Trinity Center helping drug and alcohol addicts overcome their addictions. My plan was to conduct group sessions there twice a week.

Due to my lack of childhood education, the mere thought of going to college was terrifying. In my late 40s, I took a few classes at Ivy Tech Community College but didn't do very well. I just didn't fit in with my young classmates. In my early 50s, I enrolled in a class at Indiana University, again surrounded by students much younger than me. I was completely out of place.

A few years went by, and I decided to give my education another try—this time at Indiana Wesleyan University in Marion, Indiana. I had met a young lady who was enrolled there; she suggested I accompany her to a class. I took her up on her offer, and we drove to Marion twice a week. I enjoyed the atmosphere but lacked direction. I found out Saint Joseph's offered classes to anyone wanting to work in the addiction field, so I quit Indiana Wesleyan.

I decided to offer a workshop on cutting and coloring hair and how to do nails for a $10 fee. One day, one of my vendors came by my house to deliver my order, and as we chatted, she told me she was enrolled in Indiana Wesleyan's adult student program.

"They hold class once a week and host study groups for students who are struggling," she said.

When I asked what subjects she was required to take, she ran out to her car and grabbed her lessons to show me. To my surprise, the classes she was taking were the same ones I had completed and passed at Saint Joseph's.

That day, I decided to enroll at Indiana Wesleyan University. The vendor helped me complete the paperwork, and we became good friends. I went to school every Thursday from 6 p.m. to 10 p.m., the same hours I worked at

General Motors.

After enrolling in school, I told my co-worker, Abby, about my new journey. Abby offered to cover for me Thursday evenings while I was in class, so I notified all my supervisors to contact her on the days I was out. My daughter also enrolled at Indiana Wesleyan, and we carpooled to Indianapolis. Four years later, we graduated together—me at fifty-seven and my daughter at thirty-seven.

Until then, I had spent most of my life being what others wanted me to be so they would accept me. Many young Blacks today don't understand why we didn't stand up for ourselves against racism back then. What people have to understand is that we were trying to get our piece of the American dream. We wanted better jobs, new homes, new cars, and all the finer things in life that Whites had. As adults, we assimilated as much as possible to be accepted.

Blacks who came from poverty and a corrupt

system designed to keep us down were willing to do whatever was required to prosper and set our children up to prosper, too. Not only by basic living standards but on an educational level, as well. Back then, we believed if our children could receive a good education and were able to attend college, they would be successful. However, we didn't realize that with both parents working outside the home, our children were left home with little to no supervision. It was worse for children being raised by single parents.

Our children did have the finer things in life, way more than I had growing up. What they lacked was our attention. When children are abandoned or neglected of their parent's love, nurturing, and time, it causes emotional distress, which can lead to more serious issues, perhaps even self-medication with drugs or alcohol. They may have grown up with plenty; however, the residue of neglect produces emotionally crippled adults who continue the same cycle with their children—a curse that can last for generations.

Unfortunately, you'll find that most parents who have emotionally injured their children were emotionally injured themselves. Sadly, they don't seek the help they need to heal from their painful pasts. Instead, they go about life injuring others because they refuse to admit anything is wrong.

Most parents will never confess to raising their children the same way their parents raised them because doing so forces them to revisit their childhood. Instead, they blindly refuse to acknowledge how their suffering has affected their parenting. Without receiving help, the painful cycle continues from one generation to the next until someone finally breaks it by healing.

My emotional healing began when I met my best friends, June Jones and Naomi. Meeting them blessed my life! Not only did they become my best friends, but they also taught me how to hear from God. June always told me that God had a purpose for my pain and a plan for my life, and both women helped me through the pain. For over eight years, we met at June's house every Wednesday evening. This is how I became restored.

Emotional healing requires diving into the experiences that have hurt us. Along the way, we glean wisdom and may suffer attacks, but our commitment to changing our lives and doing the work to heal becomes stronger. During the healing journey, we learn to love and appreciate ourselves, set boundaries and limits that feel right for us, be good advocates of ourselves, build our self-esteem, and develop a list of activities that help us feel better.

Healing emotionally doesn't mean forgetting the pain. It just means the trauma no longer hurts, affects, or controls us. To let go of past hurts and pains, we must speak a positive mantra over ourselves to counter painful thoughts, create physical distance, be gentle with ourselves, and accept that those who have hurt us may never apologize for the pain they've caused. Hurt people hurt other people, so don't be surprised to find they're unaware they've done something wrong.

Emotional healing is imperative. Failing to heal emotionally leaves us operating in pain. Personally, I wouldn't be operating in God's purpose for my life without healing first. How do you know you're healing? There are several ways to know.

Getting better at recognizing and naming the emotions you are experiencing is a sign that you're healing. When things go wrong and you handle them without automatically blaming yourself, you're healing and will learn to trust yourself. No more second-guessing, ruminating, or underestimating yourself. You'll speak up without worrying and be less sensitive to rejection or slights.

I can't tell you how many women have told me how they were mentally and physically abused by their parents. Unfortunately, their parents were probably abused themselves. It's sad how many adults don't take steps to heal, refuse to admit they're not loving parents, and injure their children and others around them.

Many clients I serve at Gilead House come from backgrounds tainted with molestation, alcohol and drug abuse, and divorce. Their parents and stepparents were damaged themselves and continue the patterns of abuse. Growing up, we were poor, but I never remember ever being hungry or without heat in our home. We had just enough. In fact, as little as we had, most of our neighbors were less fortunate than us.

We live in a world where it's "acceptable" for our inner wounds to be left untreated. I believe this is because so many people (especially Blacks) ignore the signs or don't recognize they're emotionally suffering. If you're unsure if you fit in this category, ask yourself the following questions to help identify where you stand.

Are you displaying anger, agitation, anxiety, or

moodiness? Are you withdrawn or isolating yourself from others? Poor self-care or perhaps engaging in risky behavior such as drugs and alcohol? If you feel hopeless, worthless, or overwhelmed, these are all signs of emotional suffering.

God Dealing with My Sorrows

I am pledging the last years of my life to God! I feel awful about how I have treated God. Like I am a fraud! I teach others to overcome their addictions; however, I have not fully recovered from my addiction to food. I've allowed sweets and bread to replace God in my life. Even as I write this, God allowed me to feel the pain that He feels every time I go to Him in prayer but don't do what He says.

While waiting for God to work out my situation, I stand in the corner with the devil laughing it up, allowing my fears and emotions to control me. I tend to bury my problems beneath sweets and bread, stuffing myself with the wrong kinds of foods that have made me obese and miserable. But every time God fixed my situation, I went back to Him with gratitude. You will conquer your addiction when you give God control of it. God loves us, and He hears our prayers.

Psalm 50: 7-15 reminds us that God asks us to call on Him in times of trouble.

I have learned through my sorrows that God never abandons us during our times of hurt, pain, and grief. Instead, He provides us with His love and gives us hope. He catches every tear that falls from our eyes, and the former pain passes away. The book of Isaiah talks about how Jesus bears all our grief and carries our sorrows. Whenever I feel worthless, I remember how Jesus carried my pain, which frees me to move towards healing.

One evening after getting home from Gilead House, I decided to cross the road in my truck to check my mail. Even though it was dark outside, I took my eyes off the road long enough to look at my driveway to see if my grandson was home. As I pulled up to my mailbox, two children screamed at me from another car because I had crossed the road into their lane. I almost killed them! Thank God they swerved, and there were no other vehicles behind me. I have always prayed for God to protect me from hurting others. If anyone's life has to be taken, I would rather God take mine and spare the other person's life.

The next morning, I woke up thankful God spared those children's lives. As I gave thanks, God began speaking to me.

I protected your life by not letting you kill those children, He said. *I spared their lives for you. Now what are you going to give Me?*

I have surrendered every area of my life to God,

except for my food addiction. Right now, today, I hand it all over to Him. Lord, I give You my all! My overwhelming gratitude is to God. His gracious love, protection, mercy, and kindness that He has for me implores me to give up my addiction to food. I am willing to do whatever I have to do for the glory of God.

Addiction feels like a black cloud hanging over your head that walks with you daily. No matter where you go, that black cloud hovers over you, causing storms that leave you feeling hopeless. Overcoming any addiction seems impossible to achieve. What starts as comfort to ease your pain or something to help you unwind evolves into a nightmare you believe you'll never wake up from. It feels as if God has forsaken you—like you have no support and must fend for yourself.

I know I have failed God by entertaining the devil and his temptations. Even after God resolves the situation and I thank Him over and over for healing me, I turn around and repeat the same pattern. I have realized I don't have the faith or trust in God that I portray to others. I don't feel like a faithful Christian. From this day forward, I repent to God and intend to change my life with His help. I promise God that I will study His Word until He decides to deliver me from myself.

My neighbor used to tell me that I can't help myself; my behavior is just the way I am. That is not true! With God's help, anyone can change. You do not have to remain who you currently are or stay in the same place. You can change your life if you are willing to do the work. It all starts with you!

God promises to deliver us from the darkness of our sins. All we have to do is ask, and He will be there for us. God's love gives us the power and ability to overcome any addiction, achieve sobriety, and gain personal success. As you ask God to help you overcome addiction, you must remember these two things: God's love is amazing, and He allows us to experience suffering to grow and mature in Christ.

Psalm 46:1 reminds us that God is our shelter and strength, always there to help in troubling times.

God doesn't expect us to be perfect. He wants to help us be persistent in overcoming our sins and learn to manage our addictions with effort and sacrifice while holding on to His everlasting love. Leaning on God during our storms gives us the power to withstand any temptation to beat addiction through Christ, who strengthens us. Learning to cope with our emotions helps us overcome the difficult times as we grow emotionally and spiritually.

James 1:2-4 reminds us to find joy in tumultuous life experiences. "Dear brothers and sisters, when troubles of any kind come your way, consider it an opportunity for great joy. For you know that when your faith is tested, your endurance has a chance to grow. So let it grow, for when your endurance is fully developed, you will be perfect and complete, needing nothing."

Climbing the ladder of success looks good to those on the outside looking in, but please remember that although we have dreams and goals, God has a purpose for our lives.

Finding and pursuing your purpose is a lifelong journey that requires faith, prayer, and a personal relationship with God. Pray and ask Him to show you the plans He has for you. Once you open your heart to God, He will reveal His plan, little by little. He will never show you all at once; it is far too big! Pray and ask Him to guide your steps as He begins showing you. You can never fulfill your God-given purpose by your own strength or by using your natural gifts and talents. You must trust God, seek His will, and ask for wisdom and guidance as you continue on your journey.

"Many are the plans in a person's heart, but it is the Lord's purpose that prevails."

(Proverbs 19:21, NIV)

Halfway through college, God took me to Heaven to reveal His purpose for my life: I was to open a home for women struggling with addiction. On September 1, 2000, I opened Gilead House, offering counseling for those women. One day while in my office alone, I was suddenly stricken with fear.

What if I fail? I asked myself. *I'll be so embarrassed!*

But the call on me was greater than my fears.

God doesn't promise that we won't stumble and fall but that He will give us the strength to get back up and carry on when we do. He doesn't make a promise without guiding us to the purpose. The joy that follows discovering our purpose comes with fear. Fear has a way of paralyzing us, ushering in doubt and draining our strength, eventually causing us to question our decisions.

2 Corinthians 12:9 states, "God tells you that His strength is all you need because His power is greatest when you are weak."

When facing a decision as big as following God's purpose and plan, remember He is your strength and is there to carry you through fear and doubt.

After moving my business to three different locations in 2017, I was blessed with funding through Recovery Works of Indiana to begin offering mental health counseling. With those funds, I was able to provide housing and meals for up to twenty-seven women. Gilead House paid for all the other essentials they needed. The women were allowed to stay at Gilead House free of charge for three to four months.

As of January 31, 2021, we have been operating

for twenty-one years, and we're still going strong!

When I feel like I am not as smart as others, God reminds me that I took a word from Him and created a ministry. He reminds me that I may not know what I am doing, but He does. And He is doing all His works through me!

"Remain in me, as I also remain in you. No branch can bear fruit by itself: it must remain in the vine. Neither can you bear fruit unless you remain in me."

(John 15: 4-5)

God doesn't care that we are imperfect creatures. He embraces our flaws and encourages us to use them to draw closer to Him. As long as we trust God and stay obedient to His Word, we are not alone. Pray and ask Him for direction and guidance when you feel lost. God promises to love and support all His children and to deliver every one of us from all obstacles aimed to destroy us.

When God gives us a business plan and idea, He makes sure we have the means to successfully see them through. There is nothing better than God being a part of our accomplishments.

"Remember the Lord your God. He is the one who gives you power to be successful."

(Deuteronomy 8:18)

Our skills and talents to run businesses are given to us by God. I received a word from God, which became a ministry that gave abused, lost, and addicted women the chance to be saved, restored, and healed from their hurts and become better mothers, wives, and daughters, all because God loves them. And so do I!

Gilead House glorifies God because it imitates God's character and what He allowed to be created through me (Reba Harris). Gilead House, in all aspects of the business—including ownership, profit, money, competition, borrowing and lending—glorifies God because they are reflective of His nature.

The Vision

After leaving the Methodist church, where women were allowed to serve as pastors and leaders, I joined a Baptist church where only male leaders were in charge. Except for the children's classes, even the Sunday school teachers were male. Women were allowed to teach small children; however, men were assigned to teen classes.

I had been raised in church, and at age nineteen, I accepted Christ into my life at Wayman Methodist Episcopal Church in Kokomo, Indiana, under the leadership of Reverend Elliott, Assistant Pastor. His Bible teachings were wonderful.

Wednesday night Bible study with Reverend Elliott was fire! He never failed to let parishioners know that those who are saved go to Heaven, and those who aren't will go to hell to burn forever. Some people didn't like Reverend Elliott because they were tired of being told they were going to hell. In my opinion, we need to hear those same messages in the church today. Hearing about hell may not be a popular message among the congregation, but we need to hear that there is a place for those who don't accept Jesus Christ as their Lord and savior.

If only more people would accept Christ and change from their wicked ways, our world would be a better place to live. There wouldn't be a racial divide, and it wouldn't matter who's in the White House. The question is, are you in God's house? Are you truly living for God and not just for show? If you are truly saved by the Blood of Jesus, you will live right and not hate your brother or sister because of the color of their skin. We are all a part of God's creation. In his Word, He says do not come to Him with sin in your heart.

"If I had cherished sin in my heart, the Lord would not have listened."

(Psalm 66:18)

Chasing after men of power and our own greed is a sure way to fall into the consequences of our almighty God for turning our backs on Him. Whether we believe in God or not, He is real! And on that great day, we will have to answer to Him for every thought, word, and deed we have done. We must pray that the Blood of Jesus has covered our sins and come to God with our hearts ready to repent, asking for His forgiveness and to accept us into His kingdom. Be willing to listen and obey the voice within us and accept our God-given purpose as He reveals it to us.

We should all dare to be different. I was only nineteen when God placed a thirst for His Word in my heart. At the age of twelve, determined not to repeat the cycle of my tumultuous upbringing, I remember standing in our house, praying that God would help me be a better parent to my future kids than my parents had been to me.

When I was a little girl, I loved playing church with my brothers, Leonard and William. I made them be my helpers, commanding one to sing and the other to read the scripture before I preached. It's no wonder they didn't always like me! Of course, they loved me, but I know I was a pain, too. By the time I got saved, I realized that even though I had been pretending, I wasn't playing with God.

There I was, a young wife, soon-to-be mother, and a newborn Christian, striving to be a perfect Christian and spouse. For years, I worked hard to achieve my goals. By the time I was twenty-nine and changed from the Methodist to Baptist denomination, I had been studying the Bible almost ten years under Reverend Burton at Second Missionary Baptist Church. Ten mothers volunteered to host Bible study in our homes. Armed with charts and maps, Reverend Burton came and taught us from Genesis to Revelation as our children played in another room.

After a while, Wayman Church leaders advised me that I couldn't teach Sunday school and attend Reverend Burton's classes, too. So, I quit teaching because attending those Wednesday classes fed my hunger for the Lord.

This continued for several years until most of the mothers who were part of the group got jobs that kept them from attending or left Wayman to join Mount Pisgah Baptist Church. I knew I didn't belong at Wayman; I felt lost in the sophisticated, well-to-do congregation with their nice homes and good jobs. Some members did treat me well and took a liking to poor, uneducated me. But it wasn't enough to keep me there.

After joining Mount Pisgah and attending quite a few of their women's conferences, I was offered the privilege to teach my own class. I taught for two years before the conference president told me I couldn't do it anymore. I could tell they were bothered having to deliver such devastating news, but as it turned out, the governing church split and started different conventions. So, the job I loved was eliminated. This occurred on Friday, the first night of the conference. As upset as I was, I didn't show out. I stayed and enjoyed the weekend with my friend, Janice Purnell.

The Monday morning following that conference, I went to Janice's house and asked her to go with me to Tipton, Indiana. When she asked why, my answer probably shocked her: "We're going to start our own women's conference."

Tipton, Indiana, had a Catholic retirement center that I had visited with some of my White sisters from another church, and I knew the facility was available to rent. So, I booked it for our first annual women's retreat.

"Calling this one the first annual means there will be a second," Janice exclaimed.

I was scared but forged ahead. I chose a date that wouldn't conflict with other conferences in the area, thinking my retreat would be packed with ladies. Unfortunately, most of the women we targeted weren't willing to break away from the "church crowd." However, a few did come to support me, including ladies from Eastside Baptist Church in Indianapolis.

After we made it through the first one, the retreat was held for seven years at the same location. After year seven, God told me to find a bigger venue to host it. Out of obedience, I booked the Omni Hotel for our eighth annual women's retreat. People thought I was crazy, but folks continued to come.

After fourteen years of hosting women's conferences, one day, while sitting alone by the pool at the Omni, I heard God say, *This will be your last conference.* He instructed me to stop because He wanted me to focus on finishing college. I was relieved, but a bit of sadness swept over me when I thought about letting go of the women who had been attending the conferences faithfully. Honestly, I questioned God telling me to quit. I wasn't even sure if I was really hearing from Him or if I was just tired. Nonetheless, I notified my board and all the guests that this would be the last conference.

The final conference lasted from Thursday evening to noon Sunday. On Sunday morning, Debbie, a woman who had been incarcerated at the Howard County jail and was released from prison, came straight to the hotel to receive her deliverance. That blessed my soul!

Our guest speaker was Sister Elaine Walters. Instead of speaking on the topic that we assigned her, Sister Elaine got up and said, "God told me to speak on something different." She went on to say, "As God told Moses, it's time to get up and move away from this mountain. You have been held up in this one spot long enough."

Her words were confirmation of what God had spoken to me, and I wept. I knew God was telling me to quit. It was time to get up and move away from women's conferences.

Sister Elaine looked the women right in their eyes and explained, "Mrs. Harris has been with you long enough. Her purpose has been served."

Through a river of tears, the conferences ended right there. I was relieved to do what God had asked me to do once again.

At the time God instructed me to halt the conferences, I didn't know I was consenting to my next purpose—opening Gilead House as a place of healing for His daughters. Not long after God dropped the vision in my spirit, I started working on a plan. I was fifty-five years old, in my second year of college, and unprepared for the journey God had for me and Gilead House. But there was no turning back.

Once I committed to opening Gilead House, I was excited to share the vision with my classmates and others but was met with opposition I hadn't expected.

"That's nice, Reba," they'd say nonchalantly. Or, "Kokomo does not have a drug problem!"

I was heartbroken, especially when they flat-out refused to help and told me I would never get the vision off the ground. One time during a board meeting, one of the members told me that our meetings were nothing but a glorified Sunday school class!

Why were these comments so painful? Because no one considered the weight of all God was asking me to do. Me—a Black woman living in a small town with a huge vision from God, asking the community to help me start a home they felt we didn't need because the hospitals already had programs in place for what I planned to do. Regardless of how others responded and reacted, I moved forward while struggling to get through college.

It was time to stop talking about the vision and get to working on it. First, I contacted Judge Jessup to come on board with me. He became one of my biggest supporters. Then I recruited Jane, a classy woman had met through General Motors, as my board president. Jane immediately went into action, helping me raise $30,000 right away! Things started happening so fast that the board decided I needed an office and an assistant. I would be paid $12 an hour, and the assistant would be a volunteer. The board members told me even if we ran out of money, at least I could tell God I tried. Little did any of us know that months after my office opened, we would still be receiving donations.

Gilead House began in a three-room upstairs office with a kitchen that had been converted to a classroom. Once the location was secured, I contacted Debbie for help. I didn't know anything about setting up an office, so she came and worked all weekend to get it together. When I walked into my office Monday morning, all I could do was fall to my knees. It was done. No excuses. This would be where everything started.

I panicked. What did I know about running a business, Rolodexes, or operating multiple phone lines? Thank God Debbie volunteered to be my secretary until she got a job. Then Debbie's sister, Lorraine, offered to help me since she had lost her job at Chrysler. While waiting to return to work, she helped me out at my office.

The office was set up, and because of the generous donations received, there was enough money for Gilead House to hire Sandy Smith as an official employee, and I was promoted to Executive Director. Everything happened just in time; the women who needed our help began arriving.

Whenever you think something's too difficult for you to accomplish, remember the calling God gave you. You can never deny your calling. The call is always easy until it becomes unbearable and we give up. Deep down in my heart, I have always wanted to please God. Although I have failed many times and often struggle to keep going, I still try to live a life that is pleasing to Him.

A vision from God is a blessing many don't receive. You see, He doesn't give everyone the opportunity to witness the vision He has designed for our lives. When God gave me the vision to launch Gilead House, not only was I unsure about the vision, but doubtful about the process and work it was going to take to get everything done.

If the vision God gives you seems too safe or easy, it probably didn't come from Him. Whatever idea or vision you think you received from God may not be the vision He has for you, so it's imperative to seek after Him in prayer and fasting. The only way to receive a divine vision is to maintain a personal relationship with God, which requires resting in His presence.

Receiving your vision from God means He has

given you a clear understanding of your purpose and a snapshot of the business you may need to start or how to accomplish a short or long-term goal. Once you define what you should be doing on this earth, you'll find God giving you the help you need to tackle the problems that come with operating in your purpose.

There are seven spiritual gifts we need from God to operate in our purpose: **wisdom, understanding, counsel, fortitude, knowledge, piety, and fear of the Lord.** Let's discuss each spiritual gift.

Wisdom is the knowledge and understanding we receive from God. It gives us the ability to make decisions based on our experiences and intuition, allowing us to find success and happiness. We obtain God's wisdom by reading the Bible.

"The fear of the Lord is the beginning of wisdom; all who follow His precepts have good understanding. To Him belongs eternal praise."
(Psalm 111:10 NLT)

The *gift of fearing the Lord* grows us in wisdom. Fearing the Lord provokes obedience to God, sparking divine wisdom. The Bible tells us,

"Do not forsake wisdom, and she will protect you; love her, and she will watch over you. Wisdom is supreme; therefore, get wisdom."
(Proverbs 4:6-7)

We become wiser by trying new things. Go out and talk to people you don't know. A complete stranger can teach you something new! Travel the world and meet folks with different backgrounds and life perspectives. Avoid the easy route; if it's hard, you're most likely headed in the right direction. Doing things the easy way leaves little room to make the necessary mistakes that make us wiser.

Obtaining God's wisdom causes us to question His judgment on our lives. Fearing Him provokes the discipline to follow His instructions, which leads to the *spiritual gift of understanding*, allowing us to comprehend how we are to live as followers of Christ. Gaining understanding leads to living in truth; no matter what biblical teachings we come across, we'll understand what God's Word truly means. No conflicting messages will confuse us about how we're to live for Christ.

Once we start reading the Bible, we receive God's *gift of knowledge*, allowing us to understand the meaning of His Word, not only operating by truth but understanding that knowledge is more than just stating facts. Understanding helps us learn how to judge our lives by the *gift of counsel*—knowing the difference between right and wrong. We truly know we have obtained the gift of counsel when we choose to do what is right to avoid sin and maintain Godly values. We are all sinners, but avoiding temptation is completely up to us. God gives us free will. Choosing to do right in a world that mainly operates on doing what is wrong takes courage. Courage is the gift of fortitude.

The *gift of fortitude* helps us overcome fear. We can't fulfill God's vision by operating in the spirit of fear. Fortitude gives us the courage to stand up for what's right, even if we have to do it alone. Having the gift of fortitude will get us rejected and possibly verbally or physically abused. However, had God not given me the gift of fortitude, I do not think I would have gotten Gilead House started because many people called me crazy for taking God's word to me and developing it into a prosperous business.

With fortitude, we have the courage to do right while enduring the evil consuming this world. Once we have the courage not to live *of* the world but in the world, that is when God gives us the gift of piety or reverence. The *gift of piety* stops us from wanting to do wrong, keeps us on the path of righteousness, and gives us a deep respect for God to come before Him with humility, trust, and love. The gift of piety activates the Holy Spirit within us, where we worship and obey God.

If you are unsure about life, what you are supposed to be doing, or are uncertain who you are, the best solution I have is for you to learn who you are so God can reveal your purpose for still living on this earth. Pray and ask God to give you a vision by receiving the seven spiritual gifts so you can take His Word (just like I did) and serve your life's purpose.

Timeline of the Vision

A vision is the ability to dream of or plan the future with imagination or wisdom. Everyone has a vision—something we imagined for ourselves growing up as a child. Whether to become a police officer, doctor, or lawyer, we envisioned ourselves doing it before it became a reality. That's how Gilead House was started: a simple word and instructions from God. I had a vision of what the recovery home would look like and how it would be run. Once the vision became my reality, I established a vision statement.

What is a vision statement? A vision statement is the roadmap that gives your business direction to its destination. Constructing one provides a sense of purpose and establishes short- and long-term goals for your business.

The Gilead House Vision

One morning while stopped at a red light in front of Central School, I noticed a young girl sitting on the curb in front of the Memorial Gym on Apperson Way. Though her head was down, I recognized her from the community and knew she was struggling with addiction. I also knew her children were living with their grandparents.

This young lady was a crack addict. The sun was rising, and once again, she had to face a difficult day. The vision of her sitting there was devastating.

Weeping, I told God, "Your daughters are in trouble, God. What are we going to do?"

The sky opened up, and I was in the presence of God.

"I want you to open a home for My daughters," He

said. *"When you do, teach classes on healing from abortion."*

I was stunned. But God wasn't done speaking.

"My daughters won't come to Me for salvation because they have had an abortion," He said. "Tell them for Me that I have forgiven them. All I ask of them is to help other women not to do the same."

At that time, I saw women of all races and cultures walking up to a house that had come down from the sky.

"God, I don't want to do this because non-profits never have any money," I said.

"When others around you are closing, and they ask you how you are staying open..." An arm emerged from the sky, and the hand touched the top of the building as God continued. "...tell them I have My hand on your place."

Real People, Real Change, Real Results!

Reba Harris

The Call:
Outreach to women with substance abuse addictions.

The Vision:
A safe haven for women and their pre-school children.

History:
May 1997 – The first steering committee met to establish a board.

August 11, 1997 – Letters were sent out to prospective board members.

September 8, 1997 – Officers were elected; the constitution and by-laws were accepted.

October 6, 1997 – Reba Harris was hired as Executive Director of Gilead House. Areas of need were addressed, and committees were formed.

December 2, 1997 – Reba discussed the difficulty of getting the 501c3 non-profit status.

January 6, 1998 – People in the community were recruited to work on helping us obtain our 501c3 status. Country tax preparer, Delmo Lynch, agreed to assist us with the non-profit status, along with Attorney Corbin King.

April 4, 1998 – We received our tax-exempt status.

November 17, 1998 – We received our 501c3 non-profit status.

January 5, 1999 – New officers were elected; Jayne Deno was elected board president.

April 25, 2000 – We launched weekly programs with Howard County Jail's female inmates.

On September 1, 2000, the doors to Gilead House opened at 608 East Boulevard Street, Kokomo, IN, offering services to females eighteen years and older, with future plans to provide

115

housing for addicts and their children until they attained sobriety and the necessary skills to help them become productive members of society. We were blessed with fourteen acres of property to complete this task. However, since the land was inconvenient to places of business that residents needed access to, we were told by city authorities that we couldn't utilize the property for our site.

Our plans changed from looking for land to build on to searching for a space to accommodate women who needed housing, substance abuse classes, life/skill classes, and mental health services—a search that would take several years. In the meantime, we served women from several different spaces.

Moving from our first location to two subsequent ones helped us gain additional space to serve the women coming for help, but we were in tremendous need of funding for the right locale. At the time, Gilead House was operating on donations from the community and a few grants.

We visited many sites that were potential matches for our vision, but none of the buildings were in the condition we needed.

In 2013, Mr. John O'Donnell called me to come over and look at the women's YWCA. It had sat vacant for a few years. Again, I was too scared to be excited that we had possibly found our new home. The thought of supervising and maintaining a 20,000-square-foot facility was terrifying! I turned down the offer. A year went by, and two of our generous donors, John and Patty O'Donnell, asked about the possibility of revisiting the YWCA.

"Are you going to move forward or go backwards?" John said. "Patty and I will be with you, just as we have been in the past."

Reluctantly, I agreed, and the O'Donnells wrote a check that paid for the building!

John handed me the keys with a smile and said, "Keep doing what you are doing!"

In the fall of 2014, the old YWCA became the

new home for Gilead House. As we moved in, my mustard seed-sized faith superseded any fear and doubt I had. Nearly twenty-two years later, we are still operating strong, with twenty-five women continuing their addiction treatment.

To God be the glory!

Evolution of the Gilead

The vision of Gilead House is to be a substance abuse treatment center of choice for women. I walked around with the vision in my head for a long time. I did not know what had happened, but one Sunday while in church, I read in the Bible where God said to Isaiah, "Will you go?" Isaiah replied, "I will go!" God spoke to me again and said, "Will you go?" I started crying because I knew it was God asking me to do Him a favor.

He had told me it would not profit my family;

I would not get rich off the project. He said, "I just need you to do me a favor. I need a place where my daughters can come and get their hurts healed, and hopefully, they will come to accept me and become better women and mothers to their children." When the God of the universe asks you to do Him a favor, it makes you want to say yes, even though you may be afraid of failing.

Saying yes to God is the most important decision you will ever make. Your "yes" means being who He wants you to be and becoming all you can for Him. It means living in your purpose with God leading the way and believing He will do exactly what He said He would do. Your "yes" to God allows Him to show you the great plans He has for you. You will experience healing and freedom from guilt and sin. As I said before, God gives us free will. He doesn't force His plans on us; He patiently waits for our "yes."

Whether out of fear or the desire to live on their terms, many people do not give God their "yes."

Whatever the reason for rejecting God's plan for our life and living by our own rules, fleshly desires will cause us to die by those same desires. The Bible makes it clear the wrong choice leads to death.

"For the wages of sin is death, but the free gift of God is eternal life through Jesus Christ our Lord."
(Romans 6:23)

The good news is we do not have to die! Saying yes to God automatically gives us life; becoming part of His family connects us deeply to Him.

Nehemiah told God yes when he agreed to help God build the wall in Jerusalem.

"Who was led to build a wall around a city to protect the people in the city, the builders were met at first with ridicule. The builders were called feeble Jews. It was said that perfumers and goldsmiths have no muscles."

(Nehemiah 4:1-6)

121

When Nehemiah told God that he would rebuild the wall, he didn't know how long it would take him or how big, long, or wide the wall would be. He didn't ask God how many times the wall had been built around Jerusalem. I'll even go so far as to say he never even knew if a wall had been built around Jerusalem before. Nehemiah didn't care. All he knew was when he told God yes, God would supply all his needs to rebuild the wall.

I felt like Nehemiah when God was calling me to open Gilead House. After all, the city already had two treatment centers. So, I was bound to be met with resistance, right?

My first encounter with ridicule came shortly after I began telling people that God had taken me to Heaven and showed me the vision for Gilead House. "You're nothing but a factory worker. All you're good at is building radios for General Motors," some said. Others told me, "You aren't smart enough to do something like that!"

I encountered the same problems and ridicule as Nehemiah, like the officials of Tekoa refusing to cooperate with him and how Sanballat and Tobiah ridiculed him. *(Nehemiah 3:5)* He even received threats of violence from his enemies. *(Nehemiah 4:7-8)* All the obstacles Nehemiah experienced were traps to delay the mission God had given him to accomplish. Nehemiah's story made me realize the ridicule thrown at me was only an attempt to stop me from doing what God called me to do.

Our "yes" doesn't mean God will ask us to do anything for our benefit or gain. Why would God ask us to do something only we will benefit from? God has never asked me to do anything for Him that I felt comfortable doing. He just said what He needed me to do, and I said YES. Many people assumed I opened Gilead House to make money since I had retired from General Motors. Some folks went as far as to suggest I should keep working there or go home and babysit my grandchildren while their parents worked.

Oscar said, "I thought when you retired, you were just going to stay home with me."

Yes, even my own husband was part of the ridicule.

My "yes" had negative effects on my marriage. One day while at a retreat in Muncie, I told a pastor my testimony about how Gilead House came to be, and he asked me had I asked for my husband's approval to do what God had asked me to do. I shook my head and told him I hadn't asked Oscar's permission.

The pastor startled me when he said, "If your husband does not want you to carry out the vision, you should not do it."

"God knew I had a husband when He asked me to carry out His vision," I responded, staring right in his eyes. "Don't get it twisted. My husband is not my God; he is just my husband."

Even one of my lady friends asked what I would do if Oscar threatened to leave me.

"Then he will just be gone, and I'll have an ex-husband," I replied.

Whenever I was asked how Oscar felt about me carrying out God's vision, my answer was the same: "My husband is not happy with the call God has given me."

By this time, Oscar was retired. He was hoping that when I retired, I would sit with him in our garage, watching traffic go by all day. What people need to understand is there's a voice inside us, urging us to be our true selves. When we ignore the person we are truly meant to be, that voice provokes us to negative behavior. This is where issues like addiction are bred. It's pretty rare for anyone to know or take the time to find out who God created us to be when we're young. We spend most of our lives being who others want us to be. The thing is, those roles we end up playing don't tell us who we are or what we're capable of becoming.

It would have been easier to disobey God's call

if I could've just said, "Well, my husband told me I can't open a women's shelter, so I won't do it!" I had asked a few people for their opinion about me starting a business without my husband's consent. Some of their comments made me second-guess opening Gilead House, my assignment from God. They said I shouldn't do it if Oscar wasn't in agreement. The only thing that kept me moving forth with it was God Himself. I couldn't let the vision go. Remember, God had asked little ole me to do Him a favor.

Despite his initial opposition, over time, Oscar became my biggest supporter. He consented that taking on this challenge from God meant I would be away from the house even more than I had been already. Remember, when God called me, I was still employed at General Motors and in my third year at Indiana Wesleyan University. Now here I was, telling my husband that God wanted me to open a home for women, taking more time away from him.

I realized it's not easy to believe in a person who claims they are moving on a word from God, not a whim. I added my faith to that word and started a ministry in spite of my sordid past. I was more than the poor child, wife, mother, and employee people saw me as being. In my eyes, up until that point, I hadn't accomplished anything significant with my life. Why would God want to use me for something so big?

Starting Gilead House required me to spend a lot of time around other men. It was hard because, having witnessed a fair share of infidelity, Oscar had a serious problem trusting me or anyone else. Before we got together, Oscar had dated several women. Some cheated on him, and he cheated on some. So, mistrust was a dominating factor throughout our marriage. I think this is why he died without making sure he secured life insurance to make sure I was taken care of. Sure, there was the policy Chrysler provided, but it had decreased over the years. To this day, I believe my husband's reason for not obtaining life insurance was so I wouldn't have a good time with the money that would have been left to me when he died.

I had grown up witnessing my mother's pain when my father cheated on her. As a Christian, I never wanted to commit the sin of adultery. Within the sixty-one years of our marriage, I never cheated on Oscar, nor did I have any reason to believe he was unfaithful to me. We were faithful to each other until the day he died.

People often ask me how I told God "yes" and carried out His vision. I tell them it wasn't easy. It took over five years to open the office and another seventeen to launch the residential housing program. What kept me going, even in the face of my husband mistrusting me, the community doubting me, and my lack of faith in myself, was what God said to me ringing in my ears: "I need you to do Me a favor. I need a place for My daughters to go, so they will have a chance to change."

Twenty-one years later, although fatigue has set in, I still hear from God. He told me, "I know you are tired and want to come home to Heaven. You have lost your husband and many friends who you loved dearly."

I took a deep breath and kept listening.

"I know you want to come home to Me, but what do you think is more important to Me? You coming home happy or staying at Gilead House and giving the women a chance to change? What matters to you the most?"

This was just the other day. All I could do was think about what God asked me in silence.

As I started developing Gilead House, I needed help from our community leaders, so I approached city officials for assistance.

"We already have two treatment centers," they said. "We don't need another one. Besides, we don't have a drug problem in our town."

Their criticism was extremely reminiscent of

the way Sanballat ridiculed Nehemiah in front of the Samaritan army. *Nehemiah 4:3* taught me how Nehemiah overcame the pressure. When God gives us a vision, the first thing we'll always encounter is opposition from others—even mocking and laughter.

My intimidation came from the inside. I knew I wasn't smart enough to accomplish such a daunting task. I hadn't graduated from Indiana Wesleyan yet, even though I was getting good grades. I didn't seem to be a person who God would call to do anything of this magnitude. Why would He appoint me for such a tremendous task when so many more people could do it better than me?

There was a point when Nehemiah and his followers ran out of energy. For me, this time came after two knee replacements, and we were struggling to come up with the funds to keep our employees paid on time. I always tried to pay the people who were single and had no other source of income. If I couldn't pay them right away, they were the first to get their checks when we received the money the following week.

As the program director, I didn't want anyone upset with me over payroll, so I paid some of them out of my own pocket when I could. As hard as I tried to make things right, it didn't stop the gossiping and chatter about Gilead House not being in bad condition if I were a better director.

"Now that the work had begun, the Jews were furious and very indignant."

(Nehemiah 2:19)

The nature of the attack shows that Nehemiah had to sacrifice and seek God with expectations for Him to miraculously build the wall on his behalf. Like most attacks of discouragement, there is a trace of truth in the words of the enemy.

Many nights I lay on the floor of my living room, crying out to God over not being able to do what He was asking me to do. I was embarrassed that I had failed Him and my employees. Eventually, I ran out of tears.

"God, I don't know what I am doing!" I shrieked.

"I know you don't know what you are doing, but I know what I am doing, and I am going to do it through you," He answered.

I felt much better after hearing His voice; however, it didn't dissolve some of my staff's bitterness and rude behavior.

The enemy uses discouragement to attack our faith in God. Faith allows us to believe God's Word and what He says. When you feel discouraged, you believe the worst will happen and start forgetting God's promises.

"Of rumors, of attacks, but Nehemiah reminded them that the Lord will fight your battles for you and your family."

(Nehemiah 4:15-23)

The people discouraging you are the same ones who don't have a clue what God is capable of, so they often miss what He is doing.

I was caught off guard when my board president advised me that the staff was demanding to speak to the board, claiming I was getting senile, didn't know what I was doing, and that the city was aware I was incompetent and should be fired. According to them, Gilead House needed to hire another director who could bring in more money.

"Sanballat and Tobiah had no authority to actually stop the work. All they could do was to discourage the Jews into stopping."

(Nehemiah 2:7)

My board members were trying to discourage me from quitting the vision God had given me years ago. I had to strengthen my faith, trust, and belief in Him in order to make it through.

At the meeting, the board president told the employees, "Reba has admitted she has made some mistakes, but she's not going anywhere. If you don't want to continue working under her supervision, you're welcome to seek employment elsewhere."

The staff agreed to stay on, but the fight wasn't over. The last straw was when an employee started a new class at Gilead House without informing me. When I confronted her about it, her answer dumbfounded me: "I didn't think you had anything left to offer Gilead House."

I stormed off to my office and asked God to remove the employees who couldn't stay on this journey with me. "Let them think it was their idea to leave," I prayed, and God answered my prayers.

"A new problem came up for Nehemiah and his followers they ran out of food. There was a famine in the land."

(Nehemiah 5:1-5)

The Gilead House had gone through the economy failing, factories closing, and patrons saying they couldn't donate to us the way they had before because they had to provide for their families—even their grown children. In 2020, the world was introduced to COVID 19, a vicious disease that brought violent sickness, death, job losses, community shut-downs with no face-to-face gatherings or events, and a fear of what was happening to our world. The Gilead House has been affected by all of these things, in addition to caring for residents who have been stricken with the virus and quarantined at the facility.

The resistance has been external and internal, but through it all, the Gilead House still provides women with the help they need each and every day. Their lives are changing, and they're reclaiming their roles as mothers as they heal from their damaged lives and work to become better people, mothers, and women of God.

Nehemiah's solutions were practical,

accompanied by prayer. However, he had no solutions for the conflict of interest. Did he complete his calling? Yes, he did. The wall began (*Nehemiah 3:1*). It was halfway completed (*4:6*). Except for the gates, it was erected (*6:1*), completely finished (*6:15*) and dedicated (*12:27*).

Christians are called to fulfill God's purpose in His Kingdom. Are you listening for your call? We don't get to select our audience. Only God can do that for us. Our job is to say yes. *Lord, yes!* Send me, and I will go.

The Sorrows of Addiction

(THE FOLLOWING ARE STORIES OF HOW AND WHY SOME PEOPLE START USING DRUGS AND ALCOHOL.)

Fifteen-year-old Betsy was molested and impregnated by her own brother. When her mother found out, she forced Betsy to have an abortion. A few years later, Betsy was raped by her mother's boyfriend and became pregnant a second time. Again, Betsy's mother found out and forced her to have another abortion.

This painful cycle of abuse continued over a long period. Betsy was so ashamed and lonely that she started searching for something to ease the pain consuming her. She started drinking alcohol to cope and enjoyed its lasting effect. Not only did getting drunk make her feel better, but it also helped Betsy forget why she was hurting.

As the years passed, Betsy slowly became addicted to alcohol. Every day she drank, her body becoming numb to the effects the alcohol had on her. She started feeling the same whether she drank or not. She had to find something stronger to help her cope with the residue from years of abuse. Craving something to help stop the pain, Betsy mixed marijuana with her alcohol. Using both drugs and alcohol caused the pain and hurt to subside. It made her numb to the abuse of her past.

The more Betsy used, the more her body became immune to both the marijuana and alcohol. Nothing seemed to stop the burning pain on the inside of her. Since her drugs of choice were no longer helping Betsy cope, she turned to sex. She believed being promiscuous with various men would help her find the love she so desperately wanted and needed from her parents, but it didn't stop her from feeling like she was dying inside. So, Betsy began cutting herself. Cutting canceled the pain of the molestation, rapes, abandonment, and rejection issues she experienced from her birth mother.

After years of harming herself with destructive behavior and being sent to prison several times, nothing seemed to end the darkness in Betsy's dismal life. The pain, shame, and hurt grew to be unbearable. Not even becoming a mother gave her the feeling of being loved she desired. The burdens finally became so heavy for her to carry that Betsy tried to commit suicide.

When tragedy strikes, many of us ask, "Why did God let me be born?" "Why didn't my parents love me?" "What's wrong with me?" I'm sure Betsy did the same. However, at forty-four years of age, Betsy gave her life to Christ! Through Christ, she learned not only to forgive others but, most importantly, God helped her learn to forgive and love herself. She knows that through Christ, she is fearfully and wonderfully made. God has given her another chance at this thing called life.

At thirteen, Molly was walking home from school with a group of girlfriends, just like any other normal teenage girl would do. What made Molly different from the other girls was that while her friends chattered like typical teens on the long walk, Molly was praying. She wasn't praying for just anything, though. Molly prayed that her mother would be home when she arrived.

"Dear Lord, please let Mommy be home when I get there. And if she is there, will You please let her be awake and not passed out on the couch? In Jesus' name, Amen."

As soon as she walked through the door, Molly knew her prayers hadn't been answered yet again. She entered the living room to find her mother passed out on the couch—an ordinary day for them.

By the house's messy condition, her mother had been passed out most of the day. The curtains were closed, the house was dark and smelled like alcohol, and it was musty. Molly dreamt of food cooking on the stove every day when she got home so she would have something to eat. Sadly, the aroma of a delicious meal wasn't there.

Though she was there physically, Molly's mother wasn't mentally present. Her father was there, too, but he didn't make much of a difference. When he came home from work, he didn't stop to talk with her about her day at school or show any concern about her wellbeing. He just walked into the house and went straight upstairs to the bedroom. Molly felt alone.

She rummaged through the refrigerator and cabinets, trying to find herself something to eat. Some days, she gave up and went to her room without eating and cried herself to sleep.

Unable to get the love she desired from her parents, as Molly grew older, she searched for it outside of her home, dating any man she believed would love her. She ended up in a relationship with a boy from her school and spent most of her time at his house or with other friends, sometimes not returning home for weeks at a time. No one ever came looking for Molly or showed concern about her whereabouts.

Spending so much time at her boyfriend's house was Molly's way of coping with the hurt she felt from not receiving the love she desired from her parents. The more time she spent with her boyfriend, the more she picked up his bad habits. He gave her alcohol and pills that made her pass out. On numerous occasions, Molly woke up after being passed out and realized her underwear was off, and her boyfriend was lying next to her sleeping.

Molly knew she was being raped, but the drugs her boyfriend pumped into her made her not care.

All she wanted was more drugs and alcohol to numb the pain when she thought of how her parents abandoned her. Eventually, the pills weren't enough to make Molly forget; she needed something stronger to help her cope. So, Molly turned to methamphetamine and heroin.

Molly was spiraling out of control fast. She was failing in school and was never home, but her mother was too drunk to notice she wasn't there, and her father didn't care. By the time Molly turned sixteen, she was a full-blown addict. She overdosed several times and nearly died, and no one bothered to help her.

Molly's story has no ending. She's still an addict, living on the streets. A promiscuous woman, she s up with whoever will have sex with her and give her drugs. Molly knows if she continues using, she may die someday. She's afraid of dying but uses drugs to deal with the pain.

Mary grew up in a home with her parents and older sister. Her mother and father had been married for several years; her mother was a busy college student working to obtain her bachelor's degree, and her father worked long hours. Since Mary's parents were away from home for long stretches of time, she and her sister often were left with their grandfather on their father's side.

Mary's grandfather began molesting her when she was four years old. It was years before anyone knew. As Mary got older, she struggled to confide in anyone about what was happening. Initially, she thought the things her grandfather did to her were normal, until her sister confessed he had been doing the same to her.

Unexpectedly, Mary's parents announced they were getting divorced. When they said they were separating, Mary's sister told their mother about their grandfather molesting them. Now, it made sense. Mary dealt with the trauma by cutting herself and smoking marijuana. Her mother noticed the cuts on Mary's arms and her failing grades in school but assumed Mary was doing it for attention.

Mary started smoking marijuana at eleven years old. Some days, Mary would be so high that she passed out for hours. Her parents ignored her behavioral issues. There were several times when the family was prepared to go on an outing, and Mary would be passed out in her room instead of joining them. No one checked on her or seemed concerned that she was missing. As Mary grew older, she realized her family wasn't really a family. They were just people who shared the same house.

After her parents' divorce was final, Mary's father became an alcoholic and withdrew from her and her sister's lives. Their mother stayed in college and got involved in another relationship, so she still didn't spend time with her girls. Mary's marijuana addiction grew worse. Her body became immune to the marijuana, and it wasn't helping numb her pain. So, Mary turned to meth.

It was Mary's new girlfriend who introduced her to meth. Although Mary was using drugs to numb her pain, her girlfriend was her peace…until the relationship started going bad. The girls ended up homeless, causing stress between them. When the problems got worse, Mary knew the two of them needed to split, but she couldn't go live with her mother. Moving in with her father wasn't an option, either. Meth was no longer enough to help her cope, so she started using heroin.

The first time Mary used heroin, she felt like it was the love she had been looking for all her life. Being homeless, sleeping in dumpsters, and having nowhere to lay her head at night increased her thirst for a hit. She didn't have the money to fuel her heroin habit, so she stole from anyone she could to get it. Her addiction ended up getting the best of her. She sold her body for drugs and did whatever she had to do to feed her habit.

For years, nothing was done when the truth came out about Mary's grandfather molesting her and her sister. After all, he was a pastor of a church. The church demoted him, but he wasn't asked to step down, nor was he fired or punished. Mary's grandmother, who Mary loved dearly, said the two sisters were lying and never spoke to them again. To this day, she won't allow them to come around her.

Today Mary is clean due to being in a safe, sober house. Her new girlfriend is there in the house with her, but Mary doesn't know if they're going to make it once they return to the outside world. The pain Mary's grandfather inflicted on her for years has taken its toll. She doesn't want men in her life and being gay comes with its own set of problems. In Mary's words, "I don't know what my future will be. Only God knows."

Signs of Addiction

- Changes in personality and behavior like a lack of motivation, irritability, and agitation
- Bloodshot eyes and frequent bloody noses
- Shakes, tremors, or slurred speech
- Changes in their daily routines
- Lack of concern for personal hygiene
- Unusual need for money, financial problems
- A change in peer group
- Careless with grooming
- Decline in academic performance
- Missing classes or skipping school
- Loss of interest in favorite activities
- Trouble in school or with the law
- Changes in eating or sleeping habits
- Deteriorating relationships with family members and friends

- Secretiveness, lying, stealing
- Repeated unexplained outings, often with a sense of urgency
- Increased alertness
- Increased energy and restlessness
- Rapid or rambling speech
- Dilated pupils
- Confusion, delusion, and hallucination
- Irritability, anxiety, gaining or losing weight, paranoia

Ways to Cope with Addiction

- Be honest with yourself and others
- Learn to relax in any situation
- Keep a daily journal
- Develop a strong support system with other recovering addicts
- Avoid situations where you are likely to relapse
- Lower your expectations of people so if they disappoint you, it doesn't cause a relapse
- Maintain emotional composure
- Alternatively expressing and distressing your emotions
- Help other addicts
- Exercise
- Meditation
- Listen to music
- Self-pep talks

Living Life After the Fires of My Sorrows

- Get a pet
- Engage in problem solving
- Reading
- Spending time with yourself alone
- Find a hobby
- Engage in spirituality
- Spend time with friends
- Avoid the H.A.L.T. symptoms_(*Hungry, Angry, Lonely, and Tired)*

CPSIA information can be obtained
at www.ICGtesting.com
Printed in the USA
JSHW030439220822
29562JS00003B/13